Pet Vaccination
RECORD BOOK

Personal Details

NAME: --

ADDRESS: --

PHONE: ---

EMAIL: ---

Log Book Details

LOG START DATE: ---

LOG END DATE: ---

LOG BOOK NO: --

Veterinarian Information

NAME: --
ADDRESS: ---
PHONE: ---
EMAIL: ---

Pet Clinic Information

NAME: --
ADDRESS: ---
PHONE: ---
EMAIL: ---

Others Information --

Pet Vaccination History

Pet Name: _____   Date of Birth: _____

Location of Birth: _____   Sex:: _____

Breed: _____   Colour: _____

Breeder Name: _____   Breeder contact Info: _____

DATE	VACCINATION	AGE

Pet Vaccination History

Pet Name: _____ Date of Birth: _____

Location of Birth: _____ Sex:: _____

Breed: _____ Colour: _____

Breeder Name: _____ Breeder contact Info: _____

DATE	VACCINATION	AGE

Pet Vaccination History

Name: _____ Date of Birth: _____

cation of Birth: _____ Sex:: _____

ed: _____ Colour: _____

eder Name: _____ Breeder contact Info: _____

DATE	VACCINATION	AGE

Pet Vaccination History

Pet Name: _____   Date of Birth: _____

Location of Birth: _____   Sex:: _____

Breed: _____   Colour: _____

Breeder Name: _____   Breeder contact Info: _____

DATE	VACCINATION	AGE

Pet Vaccination History

Pet Name: _____ Date of Birth: _____

Location of Birth: _____ Sex:: _____

Breed: _____ Colour: _____

Breeder Name: _____ Breeder contact Info: _____

DATE	VACCINATION	AGE

Pet Vaccination History

Pet Name: _____   Date of Birth: _____

Location of Birth: _____   Sex:: _____

Breed: _____   Colour: _____

Breeder Name: _____   Breeder contact Info: _____

DATE	VACCINATION	AGE

Pet Vaccination History

Pet Name: _____ Date of Birth: _____

Location of Birth: _____ Sex:: _____

Breed: _____ Colour: _____

Breeder Name: _____ Breeder contact Info: _____

DATE	VACCINATION	AGE

Pet Vaccination History

Pet Name: _____ Date of Birth: _____

Location of Birth: _____ Sex:: _____

Breed: _____ Colour: _____

Breeder Name: _____ Breeder contact Info: _____

DATE	VACCINATION	AGE

Pet Vaccination History

Pet Name: _____ Date of Birth: _____

Location of Birth: _____ Sex:: _____

Breed: _____ Colour: _____

Breeder Name: _____ Breeder contact Info: _____

DATE	VACCINATION	AGE

Pet Vaccination History

Pet Name: _____   Date of Birth: _____

Location of Birth: _____   Sex:: _____

Breed: _____   Colour: _____

Breeder Name: _____   Breeder contact Info: _____

DATE	VACCINATION	AGE

Pet Vaccination History

Pet Name: _____   Date of Birth: _____

Location of Birth: _____   Sex:: _____

Breed: _____   Colour: _____

Breeder Name: _____   Breeder contact Info: _____

DATE	VACCINATION	AGE

Pet Vaccination History

Pet Name: _____   Date of Birth: _____

Location of Birth: _____   Sex:: _____

Breed: _____   Colour: _____

Breeder Name: _____   Breeder contact Info: _____

DATE	VACCINATION	AGE

Pet Vaccination History

Pet Name: _____   Date of Birth: _____

Location of Birth: _____   Sex:: _____

Breed: _____   Colour: _____

Breeder Name: _____   Breeder contact Info: _____

DATE	VACCINATION	AGE

Pet Vaccination History

Pet Name: _____   Date of Birth: _____

Location of Birth: _____   Sex:: _____

Breed: _____   Colour: _____

Breeder Name: _____   Breeder contact Info: _____

DATE	VACCINATION	AGE

Pet Vaccination History

Name: Date of Birth:

ation of Birth: Sex::

ed: Colour:

eder Name: Breeder contact Info:

DATE	VACCINATION	AGE

Pet Vaccination History

Pet Name: _____   **Date of Birth:** _____

Location of Birth: _____   **Sex::** _____

Breed: _____   **Colour:** _____

Breeder Name: _____   **Breeder contact Info:** _____

DATE	VACCINATION	AGE

Pet Vaccination History

Pet Name: _____ Date of Birth: _____

Location of Birth: _____ Sex:: _____

Breed: _____ Colour: _____

Breeder Name: _____ Breeder contact Info: _____

DATE	VACCINATION	AGE

Pet Vaccination History

Pet Name: _____   Date of Birth: _____

Location of Birth: _____   Sex:: _____

Breed: _____   Colour: _____

Breeder Name: _____   Breeder contact Info: _____

DATE	VACCINATION	AGE

Pet Vaccination History

Pet Name: Date of Birth:

Location of Birth: Sex::

Breed: Colour:

Breeder Name: Breeder contact Info:

DATE	VACCINATION	AGE

Pet Vaccination History

Pet Name: _____   Date of Birth: _____

Location of Birth: _____   Sex:: _____

Breed: _____   Colour: _____

Breeder Name: _____   Breeder contact Info: _____

DATE	VACCINATION	AGE

Pet Vaccination History

Name: _____   Date of Birth: _____

ation of Birth: _____   Sex:: _____

ed: _____   Colour: _____

eder Name: _____   Breeder contact Info: _____

DATE	VACCINATION	AGE

Pet Vaccination History

Pet Name: _____   Date of Birth: _____

Location of Birth: _____   Sex:: _____

Breed: _____   Colour: _____

Breeder Name: _____   Breeder contact Info: _____

DATE	VACCINATION	AGE

Pet Vaccination History

Pet Name: _____   Date of Birth: _____

Location of Birth: _____   Sex:: _____

Breed: _____   Colour: _____

Breeder Name: _____   Breeder contact Info: _____

DATE	VACCINATION	AGE

Pet Vaccination History

Pet Name: _____ Date of Birth: _____

Location of Birth: _____ Sex:: _____

Breed: _____ Colour: _____

Breeder Name: _____ Breeder contact Info: _____

DATE	VACCINATION	AGE

Pet Vaccination History

Pet Name: _____ Date of Birth: _____

Location of Birth: _____ Sex:: _____

Breed: _____ Colour: _____

Breeder Name: _____ Breeder contact Info: _____

DATE	VACCINATION	AGE

Pet Vaccination History

Pet Name: _____   Date of Birth: _____

Location of Birth: _____   Sex:: _____

Breed: _____   Colour: _____

Breeder Name: _____   Breeder contact Info: _____

DATE	VACCINATION	AGE

Pet Vaccination History

Name: _____   Date of Birth: _____

cation of Birth: _____   Sex:: _____

ed: _____   Colour: _____

eder Name: _____   Breeder contact Info: _____

DATE	VACCINATION	AGE

Pet Vaccination History

Pet Name: _____   Date of Birth: _____

Location of Birth: _____   Sex:: _____

Breed: _____   Colour: _____

Breeder Name: _____   Breeder contact Info: _____

DATE	VACCINATION	AGE

Pet Vaccination History

Pet Name: _____   Date of Birth: _____

Location of Birth: _____   Sex:: _____

Breed: _____   Colour: _____

Breeder Name: _____   Breeder contact Info: _____

DATE	VACCINATION	AGE

Pet Vaccination History

Pet Name: _____   Date of Birth: _____

Location of Birth: _____   Sex:: _____

Breed: _____   Colour: _____

Breeder Name: _____   Breeder contact Info: _____

DATE	VACCINATION	AGE

Pet Vaccination History

Pet Name: _____ Date of Birth: _____

Location of Birth: _____ Sex:: _____

Breed: _____ Colour: _____

Breeder Name: _____ Breeder contact Info: _____

DATE	VACCINATION	AGE

Pet Vaccination History

Pet Name: _____ Date of Birth: _____

Location of Birth: _____ Sex:: _____

Breed: _____ Colour: _____

Breeder Name: _____ Breeder contact Info: _____

DATE	VACCINATION	AGE

Pet Vaccination History

Name: Date of Birth:

ation of Birth: Sex::

ed: Colour:

eder Name: Breeder contact Info:

DATE	VACCINATION	AGE

Pet Vaccination History

Pet Name: _____ Date of Birth: _____

Location of Birth: _____ Sex:: _____

Breed: _____ Colour: _____

Breeder Name: _____ Breeder contact Info: _____

DATE	VACCINATION	AGE

Pet Vaccination History

Pet Name: _____ Date of Birth: _____

Location of Birth: _____ Sex:: _____

Breed: _____ Colour: _____

Breeder Name: _____ Breeder contact Info: _____

DATE	VACCINATION	AGE

Pet Vaccination History

Pet Name: _____   Date of Birth: _____

Location of Birth: _____   Sex:: _____

Breed: _____   Colour: _____

Breeder Name: _____   Breeder contact Info: _____

DATE	VACCINATION	AGE

Pet Vaccination History

Pet Name: _____ Date of Birth: _____

Location of Birth: _____ Sex:: _____

Breed: _____ Colour: _____

Breeder Name: _____ Breeder contact Info: _____

DATE	VACCINATION	AGE

Pet Vaccination History

Pet Name: _____ Date of Birth: _____

Location of Birth: _____ Sex:: _____

Breed: _____ Colour: _____

Breeder Name: _____ Breeder contact Info: _____

DATE	VACCINATION	AGE

Pet Vaccination History

Name: Date of Birth:

ation of Birth: Sex::

ed: Colour:

eder Name: Breeder contact Info:

DATE	VACCINATION	AGE

Pet Vaccination History

Pet Name: _____ Date of Birth: _____

Location of Birth: _____ Sex:: _____

Breed: _____ Colour: _____

Breeder Name: _____ Breeder contact Info: _____

DATE	VACCINATION	AGE

Pet Vaccination History

Pet Name: _____   Date of Birth: _____

Location of Birth: _____   Sex:: _____

Breed: _____   Colour: _____

Breeder Name: _____   Breeder contact Info: _____

DATE	VACCINATION	AGE

Pet Vaccination History

Pet Name: _____   Date of Birth: _____

Location of Birth: _____   Sex:: _____

Breed: _____   Colour: _____

Breeder Name: _____   Breeder contact Info: _____

DATE	VACCINATION	AGE

Pet Vaccination History

Pet Name: _____ Date of Birth: _____

Location of Birth: _____ Sex:: _____

Breed: _____ Colour: _____

Breeder Name: _____ Breeder contact Info: _____

DATE	VACCINATION	AGE

Pet Vaccination History

Pet Name: _____   Date of Birth: _____

Location of Birth: _____   Sex:: _____

Breed: _____   Colour: _____

Breeder Name: _____   Breeder contact Info: _____

DATE	VACCINATION	AGE

Pet Vaccination History

Name: Date of Birth:

cation of Birth: Sex::

ed: Colour:

eder Name: Breeder contact Info:

DATE	VACCINATION	AGE

Pet Vaccination History

Pet Name: _____   Date of Birth: _____

Location of Birth: _____   Sex:: _____

Breed: _____   Colour: _____

Breeder Name: _____   Breeder contact Info: _____

DATE	VACCINATION	AGE

Pet Vaccination History

Pet Name: _____   Date of Birth: _____

Location of Birth: _____   Sex:: _____

Breed: _____   Colour: _____

Breeder Name: _____   Breeder contact Info: _____

DATE	VACCINATION	AGE

Pet Vaccination History

Pet Name: _____   Date of Birth: _____

Location of Birth: _____   Sex:: _____

Breed: _____   Colour: _____

Breeder Name: _____   Breeder contact Info: _____

DATE	VACCINATION	AGE

Pet Vaccination History

Pet Name: _____   Date of Birth: _____

Location of Birth: _____   Sex:: _____

Breed: _____   Colour: _____

Breeder Name: _____   Breeder contact Info: _____

DATE	VACCINATION	AGE

Pet Vaccination History

Pet Name: _____   **Date of Birth:** _____

Location of Birth: _____   **Sex::** _____

Breed: _____   **Colour:** _____

Breeder Name: _____   **Breeder contact Info:** _____

DATE	VACCINATION	AGE

Pet Vaccination History

Name: _____

Date of Birth: _____

cation of Birth: _____

Sex:: _____

eed: _____

Colour: _____

eder Name: _____

Breeder contact Info: _____

DATE	VACCINATION	AGE

Pet Vaccination History

Pet Name: _____ Date of Birth: _____

Location of Birth: _____ Sex:: _____

Breed: _____ Colour: _____

Breeder Name: _____ Breeder contact Info: _____

DATE	VACCINATION	AGE

Pet Vaccination History

Pet Name: _____   Date of Birth: _____

Location of Birth: _____   Sex:: _____

Breed: _____   Colour: _____

Breeder Name: _____   Breeder contact Info: _____

DATE	VACCINATION	AGE

Pet Vaccination History

Pet Name: _____   Date of Birth: _____

Location of Birth: _____   Sex:: _____

Breed: _____   Colour: _____

Breeder Name: _____   Breeder contact Info: _____

DATE	VACCINATION	AGE

Pet Vaccination History

Pet Name: _____   Date of Birth: _____

Location of Birth: _____   Sex:: _____

Breed: _____   Colour: _____

Breeder Name: _____   Breeder contact Info: _____

DATE	VACCINATION	AGE

Pet Vaccination History

Pet Name: _____   Date of Birth: _____

Location of Birth: _____   Sex:: _____

Breed: _____   Colour: _____

Breeder Name: _____   Breeder contact Info: _____

DATE	VACCINATION	AGE

Pet Vaccination History

Name: Date of Birth:

ation of Birth: Sex::

ed: Colour:

eder Name: Breeder contact Info:

DATE	VACCINATION	AGE

Pet Vaccination History

Pet Name: _____   Date of Birth: _____

Location of Birth: _____   Sex:: _____

Breed: _____   Colour: _____

Breeder Name: _____   Breeder contact Info: _____

DATE	VACCINATION	AGE

Pet Vaccination History

Pet Name: _____ Date of Birth: _____

Location of Birth: _____ Sex:: _____

Breed: _____ Colour: _____

Breeder Name: _____ Breeder contact Info: _____

DATE	VACCINATION	AGE

Pet Vaccination History

Pet Name: _____   Date of Birth: _____

Location of Birth: _____   Sex:: _____

Breed: _____   Colour: _____

Breeder Name: _____   Breeder contact Info: _____

DATE	VACCINATION	AGE

Pet Vaccination History

Pet Name: _____ Date of Birth: _____

Location of Birth: _____ Sex:: _____

Breed: _____ Colour: _____

Breeder Name: _____ Breeder contact Info: _____

DATE	VACCINATION	AGE

Pet Vaccination History

Pet Name: _____   Date of Birth: _____

Location of Birth: _____   Sex:: _____

Breed: _____   Colour: _____

Breeder Name: _____   Breeder contact Info: _____

DATE	VACCINATION	AGE

Pet Vaccination History

Name: | Date of Birth:

cation of Birth: | Sex::

ed: | Colour:

eder Name: | Breeder contact Info:

DATE	VACCINATION	AGE

Pet Vaccination History

Pet Name: _____   Date of Birth: _____

Location of Birth: _____   Sex:: _____

Breed: _____   Colour: _____

Breeder Name: _____   Breeder contact Info: _____

DATE	VACCINATION	AGE

Pet Vaccination History

Pet Name: _____ Date of Birth: _____

Location of Birth: _____ Sex:: _____

Breed: _____ Colour: _____

Breeder Name: _____ Breeder contact Info: _____

DATE	VACCINATION	AGE

Pet Vaccination History

Pet Name: _____ Date of Birth: _____

Location of Birth: _____ Sex:: _____

Breed: _____ Colour: _____

Breeder Name: _____ Breeder contact Info: _____

DATE	VACCINATION	AGE

Pet Vaccination History

Pet Name: _____

Date of Birth: _____

Location of Birth: _____

Sex:: _____

Breed: _____

Colour: _____

Breeder Name: _____

Breeder contact Info: _____

DATE	VACCINATION	AGE

Pet Vaccination History

Pet Name: _____   Date of Birth: _____

Location of Birth: _____   Sex:: _____

Breed: _____   Colour: _____

Breeder Name: _____   Breeder contact Info: _____

DATE	VACCINATION	AGE

Pet Vaccination History

Pet Name: _____ Date of Birth: _____

Location of Birth: _____ Sex:: _____

Breed: _____ Colour: _____

Breeder Name: _____ Breeder contact Info: _____

DATE	VACCINATION	AGE

Pet Vaccination History

Pet Name: _____   Date of Birth: _____

Location of Birth: _____   Sex:: _____

Breed: _____   Colour: _____

Breeder Name: _____   Breeder contact Info: _____

DATE	VACCINATION	AGE

Pet Vaccination History

Pet Name: _____   Date of Birth: _____

Location of Birth: _____   Sex:: _____

Breed: _____   Colour: _____

Breeder Name: _____   Breeder contact Info: _____

DATE	VACCINATION	AGE

Pet Vaccination History

Pet Name: _____   Date of Birth: _____

Location of Birth: _____   Sex:: _____

Breed: _____   Colour: _____

Breeder Name: _____   Breeder contact Info: _____

DATE	VACCINATION	AGE

Pet Vaccination History

Pet Name: _____   Date of Birth: _____

Location of Birth: _____   Sex:: _____

Breed: _____   Colour: _____

Breeder Name: _____   Breeder contact Info: _____

DATE	VACCINATION		AGE

Pet Vaccination History

Pet Name: _____   Date of Birth: _____

Location of Birth: _____   Sex:: _____

Breed: _____   Colour: _____

Breeder Name: _____   Breeder contact Info: _____

DATE	VACCINATION	AGE

Pet Vaccination History

Name: _____ Date of Birth: _____

ation of Birth: _____ Sex:: _____

ed: _____ Colour: _____

eder Name: _____ Breeder contact Info: _____

DATE	VACCINATION	AGE

Pet Vaccination History

Pet Name: _____

Date of Birth: _____

Location of Birth: _____

Sex:: _____

Breed: _____

Colour: _____

Breeder Name: _____

Breeder contact Info: _____

DATE	VACCINATION	AGE

Pet Vaccination History

Pet Name: _____ Date of Birth: _____

Location of Birth: _____ Sex:: _____

Breed: _____ Colour: _____

Breeder Name: _____ Breeder contact Info: _____

DATE	VACCINATION	AGE

Pet Vaccination History

Pet Name: Date of Birth:

Location of Birth: Sex::

Breed: Colour:

Breeder Name: Breeder contact Info:

DATE	VACCINATION	AGE

Pet Vaccination History

Pet Name: _____ Date of Birth: _____

Location of Birth: _____ Sex:: _____

Breed: _____ Colour: _____

Breeder Name: _____ Breeder contact Info: _____

DATE	VACCINATION	AGE

Pet Vaccination History

Pet Name: _____   Date of Birth: _____

Location of Birth: _____   Sex:: _____

Breed: _____   Colour: _____

Breeder Name: _____   Breeder contact Info: _____

DATE	VACCINATION	AGE

Pet Vaccination History

Name: _____   Date of Birth: _____

ation of Birth: _____   Sex:: _____

ed: _____   Colour: _____

eder Name: _____   Breeder contact Info: _____

DATE	VACCINATION	AGE

Pet Vaccination History

Pet Name: _____ Date of Birth: _____

Location of Birth: _____ Sex:: _____

Breed: _____ Colour: _____

Breeder Name: _____ Breeder contact Info: _____

DATE	VACCINATION	AGE

Pet Vaccination History

Pet Name: _____ Date of Birth: _____

Location of Birth: _____ Sex:: _____

Breed: _____ Colour: _____

Breeder Name: _____ Breeder contact Info: _____

DATE	VACCINATION	AGE

Pet Vaccination History

Pet Name: _____   Date of Birth: _____

Location of Birth: _____   Sex:: _____

Breed: _____   Colour: _____

Breeder Name: _____   Breeder contact Info: _____

DATE	VACCINATION	AGE

Pet Vaccination History

Pet Name: _____ Date of Birth: _____

Location of Birth: _____ Sex:: _____

Breed: _____ Colour: _____

Breeder Name: _____ Breeder contact Info: _____

DATE	VACCINATION	AGE

Pet Vaccination History

Pet Name: _____   Date of Birth: _____

Location of Birth: _____   Sex:: _____

Breed: _____   Colour: _____

Breeder Name: _____   Breeder contact Info: _____

DATE	VACCINATION	AGE

Pet Vaccination History

Name: _____   Date of Birth: _____

cation of Birth: _____   Sex:: _____

ed: _____   Colour: _____

eder Name: _____   Breeder contact Info: _____

DATE	VACCINATION	AGE

Pet Vaccination History

Pet Name: _____   Date of Birth: _____

Location of Birth: _____   Sex:: _____

Breed: _____   Colour: _____

Breeder Name: _____   Breeder contact Info: _____

DATE	VACCINATION	AGE

Pet Vaccination History

Pet Name: Date of Birth:

Location of Birth: Sex::

Breed: Colour:

Breeder Name: Breeder contact Info:

DATE	VACCINATION	AGE

Pet Vaccination History

Pet Name: _____ Date of Birth: _____

Location of Birth: _____ Sex:: _____

Breed: _____ Colour: _____

Breeder Name: _____ Breeder contact Info: _____

DATE	VACCINATION	AGE

Pet Vaccination History

Pet Name: _____ Date of Birth: _____

Location of Birth: _____ Sex:: _____

Breed: _____ Colour: _____

Breeder Name: _____ Breeder contact Info: _____

DATE	VACCINATION	AGE

Pet Vaccination History

Pet Name: _____ Date of Birth: _____

Location of Birth: _____ Sex:: _____

Breed: _____ Colour: _____

Breeder Name: _____ Breeder contact Info: _____

DATE	VACCINATION	AGE

Pet Vaccination History

Name: | Date of Birth:

cation of Birth: | Sex::

ed: | Colour:

eder Name: | Breeder contact Info:

DATE	VACCINATION	AGE

Pet Vaccination History

Pet Name: _____ | Date of Birth: _____

Location of Birth: _____ | Sex:: _____

Breed: _____ | Colour: _____

Breeder Name: _____ | Breeder contact Info: _____

DATE	VACCINATION	AGE

Pet Vaccination History

et Name: _____   Date of Birth: _____

ocation of Birth: _____   Sex:: _____

reed: _____   Colour: _____

reeder Name: _____   Breeder contact Info: _____

DATE	VACCINATION	AGE

Notes

Notes

Notes

Notes

Made in the USA
Las Vegas, NV
16 October 2024

96932620R00059